Edited and Revised Physical Edition

Written By: Hunter Kimbro

If you’re struggling with your mental health, you’re not alone.

Help is available 24/7 — Call or text **988** (U.S. Suicide & Crisis Lifeline), or

text **HELLO** to **741741** (Crisis Text Line).

You matter. Please reach out.

After the End is a deeply personal and emotionally intense story that explores themes of **grief, mental illness, suicidal thoughts, emotional isolation, and trauma** in a post-apocalyptic backdrop. While the world within the book is fictional, the emotional weight behind many scenes stems from real-life experiences and struggles.

This book includes:

- Depictions of **suicidal ideation and suicide**

- Internal monologues reflecting **self-hatred and hopelessness**
- Themes of **loss, abandonment, depression**, and **emotional numbness**
- Brief mentions of **substance misuse**
- Scenes of **violence and rage** tied to emotional breakdown

The intention of this story is not to glorify pain, but to **bring honesty to it**—to reflect the inner battle so many face silently, and to create a space where readers feel seen, even in their darkest moments.

If you're currently in a vulnerable place, please read with care.
And remember: **you're not alone.**
Resources are included at the end of the book if you or someone you know needs support.

CONTENTS

How After The End Came To Be

I began writing this book from a place of despair, sorrow, sadness whatever we want to label it. This book attempts to take my own emotions and craft them into our character

Ryan. I chose the post-apocalyptic world because i've always been fascinated with how characters are developed in those particular backgrounds, Some of Ryan's Journey and thoughts closely resemble mine from the day to day basis of writing this book. Starting in november of 2024 and now wrapping up in april the book isn't long at all. But I wanted it to feel real. I didn't want to cheat someone who spent their time reading this with a long drawn out story that did not focus on the core reasons that brought me to writing this book in the first place. In the future I plan to carry Ryan's story out in a more traditional sense that adds more characters, more places and more things to accomplish. For now I ask that you go into this story looking into the depth that I hope it brings. My Goal is that this book reaches people who feel alone in this life, and maybe just maybe you feel seen in some way. I do want to stress that this book goes through some very graphic scenes with suicide being one of them. Please know that your life is valuable and ending it is not the answer, you do matter and there are ways to reach out for help.

Enjoy

CHAPTER 1 *The World Is Yours*

Did you ever think when we were watching all these stupid movies that something like this would ever happen? I let out a small laugh. My Sense of humor was one of the small things that I held onto, even when the world fell apart. “Well um” Ted paused and seemingly looked around the thin cool air of the

Night searching for an answer. “Hell, I guess not” Ted finished. It's odd to say but I have been enjoying,

The nighttime especially since I met Ted, maybe it was just the company of what appeared as a normal person.. I peered off into the night sky

letting my thoughts and ideas run rampant like usual. It was almost like my therapy, a way to just “figure” it out,

Suddenly I let out a quick gasp that grabbed Ted's attention. Although thinking in silence helped me at times it could quickly get me shaken up too. “What going on?” Ted hastily asked “Oh uh.. it's nothing I'm fine just..thought I saw something" responding quickly so I wouldn't have to let Ted know that I had a mini panic attack. The world as I knew it was gone and that thought alone could make anyone go crazy. But no matter what I wanted to see through the destruction, the warfare I wanted to see through the terrible shit that people were doing to each other just to get by. I won't lie or pretend to be the perfect person or the shining knight in white armor because only god knows what I've also done to make it this far.

CHAPTER 2.

It had only been three days since I met Ted. We were both on the run from the constant gunfire of the major Tennessee Factions. It's funny to me that these groups of people could see everything we know and love destroyed by war just to continue it at a much smaller scale. After all, wiping out the electrical grid and more than half of the population wasn't enough to find different solutions to their disagreements. I had gotten word from an "outsider" days before I left that something was brewing between the two groups, not wanting to be around and help with another worthless killing I decided to leave. After all the group I claimed to were warmongers hell-bent on taking whatever they could just to come back home and share the bread that they never had to kill for in the first place. As for the other side well my group had met a match made in hell. 2 sides that didn't care who or why all they knew was that one had something the other didn't. While leaving that group I walked for days holding onto the hope that somewhere somehow people still cared about upholding what is right. That was when I met Ted, Ted was from the opposite side a middle-aged man seemingly in search of the same things that I was looking for. Our first exposure was a run-down gas station withholding inside nothing but a glimpse into the final days of our normal world. Seeing the chaos of products that used to sit neatly on the shelf reduced to nothing but mere rubble gave me a feeling of lost hope. As I went to make a pallet to get some rest a man appeared from behind the checkout desk holding a long barrel 22 caliber revolver. My heart sank just knowing that my final moments were upon me. “There is no need to do this” I blurted out the adrenaline-imposed response hoping that he would reason with me. The man crept closer towards me seemingly hesitant to get too close. he replied to me “Who are you and what do you want from here" Giving a stuttered yet quick response I told him "I'm just here to get some rest ok? That's all, I will leave" The man lowered the gun but kept his distance. A brief feeling of relief came over me. I had seen many people be killed without question. I knew at that moment the man was just safeguarding himself and that he also meant no harm. I slowly came up from my cardboard sleeping bag with my hands clear still hoping that he wouldn't change his mind last minute. "I'm just here for rest I promise I mean no harm to you" I assured him. He looked down at my bag seemingly looking for a weapon. "If you move towards that bag I will kill you," he told me as he looked into my eyes I could see the desperation of a man who didn't want to resort to taking my life. This intense meeting went on for what felt like hours usually it's best to not talk about where you are from but for the sake of finding common ground I told the man how I even ended up in this run-down gas station. Fast Forward 3 days later and now a Marauder and a Journeymen are sitting around a fire talking. Finding common ground and trust while running from the evils that now seemed to be behind them. I never thought in my wildest dreams that I would ever be able to reason with a member of the journeymen as sure as Ted thought the same from a Marauder. I found solace in Ted and talking about our experiences brought us all the closer as friends and now travelers. During our few nights together we would take turns feeding the flame that kept our warmth at night and this night was my turn to wake up and make sure we didn't freeze to death. But oddly Ted insisted that he would take care of the chore for tonight adding that I would love to get the extra sleep. weren't looking for a fight..and that's another valuable currency to have" "I may not know you completely but I can seAs we lay down for the night I looked up into the ceiling of the gas station watching the flames illuminate and dance off and on from the broken particle boards.I then turned to my side and asked Ted "How did you manage to keep your humanity in all of this?" it was a question I asked myself a lot. Ted continued to rip up old stock boxes "Well in today's time buddy I think doing what's right is more valuable than the dollar was," I thought on his answer which was right up the ally way of an old mentor part of the reason why I loved ted was his old school metaphors and responses he had ready to go at any time. "But why not shoot me you could have easily guaranteed yourself safety" I continued to dive deeper hoping that I could work up the courage to tell Ted about my own struggles without him seeing me in a different light. "Well buddy I could ask you the same question," Ted replied. "Look I saw that you e the hope you have…no matter what buddy if you do not have hope then you don't have nothing" ted Somley laughed at his response before tossing another piece of cardboard into the small burn barrel. I decided to take what Ted said and end the conversation there. Pondering on people's thoughts helped me get to sleep quicker so I told Ted goodnight and began to doze off. It was normal for me to have nightmares and right on cue they came. It was often nice to see my family again although the beauty never lasted long and I would soon be greeted by the same scene in which they met their fate. But just for a moment I got to see them all again, see them dancing and laughing just having fun. It was a reminder that wherever they were, it had to be a better place than here. Quickly I woke up but not from my night terrors a gunshot had rang out echoing off the walls of the empty gas station. I grabbed my gun from my waist preparing for whatever lurked in the shadows. Frantically I scanned the scene of our sleeping area and saw that Ted was nowhere to be found …..

Chapter 3

I began moving slowly throughout the gas station with my gun drawn and my heart pumping. As I swept through the main shop floor seeing nothing more than the usual rubble and trash that covered the floor. From the corner, an open door stuck out it led to the bathroom and I could see what appeared to be a dimly lit candle flashing off the tile floor. Continuing a slow approach I peered around the open door where I could see a man sitting there. “Ted” I called out. Waiting a few moments for a response which did nothing but further the amount of stress I was under. Moving forward into the bathroom I grabbed the candle and using it as my light source revealed a lifeless body. It was Ted. My heart sank as I saw the blood that now covered the side of his face, looking down at his motionless hand sat the same 22. Revolver he had used to confront me at our first meeting. Seeing the man I had become so fond of in this state sent shockwaves through my body i began to breathe frantically in a state of panic that seemed to fight the truth of what had happened to Ted. Quickly I stood up and began to search around from behind the bathroom door. Every step I took was greeted by the mashing of leftover glass and the solemn sounds of my pounding heart took an ambient noise to the leftover silence. I was sure that someone else was lurking in this gas station that we had called home. My Fear started to fade, being replaced with teeth-grinding rage. I stepped out from the open door frame beginning my descent into the darkness of the gas station. The anger fueled A moment where the realities of life and death were no more. All that mattered was finding the killer and avenging the death of the man I called a friend ignoring the dangers to myself. I stepped quickly through the dark room and began to call out to whatever lurked nearby “You motherfucker show yourself!” I began to clear all the vantage points that me and ted had marked out from our first night together. Moving closer to the stocking room I heard the sound of a box falling from its resting place onto the floor. Without an ounce of hesitation, I burst into the room and began firing. The intensity of the ringing filled my ears as flashes from my handgun's muzzle provided brief glimpses into what the room withheld. Before I knew it I had emptied the magazine into nothing more than a void. No one was there. I turned around and rushed from the stocking room back to Ted entering the bathroom for a second time just to still see what I didn't want to believe. The dawn sun was starting to creep in revealing more of teds fate and beside him I could see a folded piece of cardboard that read “Ryan”. .Briefly opening the folded cardboard letter the first sentence revealed that the man who took teds life was….ted. I closed the letter to cover my eyes all I could do was fall in defeat. Tears began streaming down my face. The very man who gave me hope seemingly had none left for himself. I tucked away the cardboard letter in my pockets and just sat there with him. It was a surreal moment that made me reflect back on whether I should have opened up my own emotions to him instead of keeping them hidden. “What have I done” The thought ran in my head over and over that if I had just opened up my true sorrows to Ted maybe he would've never felt alone…or weak in his own thoughts. Beginning to move my head up towards the ceilings as if I was looking to god for the answers just to drop right back down searching for my own. The rising sun had now completely shown itself to the world signifying that a new day was here, wiping the steady tears I got up from the floor looking one last time at my lost friend. The Marauders saw burying the dead as a waste of time, usually just dragging the bodies outside of the fences to be burned or thrown into the wilderness because “Mother Nature has to eat too” something thorne always stressed to us while we left behind our fallen looters. I never believed in that but when you're prosecuted for questioning the leader sometimes silence is the best option…well the only option. I walked outside to begin searching for the proper ground to bury Ted wanting to make sure his final resting place was something I could visit again, the backside of the gas station had a beautiful array of trees that seemingly served as an umbrella for the path leading into the woods. Off to the side stood a dogwood tree, although its flowers were not showing due to the winter I knew it would show its beautiful purity in the spring. In a world before chaos and destruction, I would always hear stories from my grandmother, about how the dogwood tree was used to make the cross Jesus was crucified on, and how god was upset with the use of the tree so he made sure that the trees never grew straight again. Giving them the true purity they deserved. I brought Ted outside, wrapping him in my square stitched blanket making sure he was comfortable before lowering him down into his true last resting place. Part of me didn't want to leave his gravesite, so many thoughts filled my mind while I stood there looking at the freshly packed dirt. Almost as if a knife was being dug into my stomach pulling at everything inside of me to find the correct answers. The worst is not a question, but a “what if?”. A glimpse into what could have been, and the reality of what will never be.

Chapter 4

I waited until the next morning to set back out from the gas station. The path forward was more clouded than the day I escaped from the marauder camp. It would be a lie for me to say I wanted to get back on the road again when in reality all I wanted to do was sleep, teds death had taken a toll that I hadn't felt since the world came crashing down. Yeah, those awful days when the men in suits decided to let hell loose. I could remember the service announcement and the eerie feeling of that robotic voice when it told us we were under attack. Watching cities fall under the siege of bombs while America prepared for its final stand. I gripped the straps of my backpack tightly forcing myself to stop thinking about it, I couldn't afford to loathe about what had happened. Looking up from my feet to see the long winding highway ahead of me I knew that it wouldn't be too much longer before I reached the Alabama State line. just the thought of getting there made me somewhat happy, after all, it was home and I hadn't been back since the great war. "God I hope this isn't a mistake" whispering to myself as the sign came into sight. With each step, I could feel the waves of uncertainty come over me, leaving guaranteed meals behind for a shot at a semi-normal life that was unheard of. I stopped in my tracks as the "Sweet Home Alabama" sign came within arms reach, it was pretty faded now no longer under upkeep by the workers who had helped make the world go around. Running my fingers across the bottom of the rusted sign gave me chills. I was home. A place my family never abandoned even as the world went to shit. "You motherfuckers" shaking my head in sarcasm, wishing those hardheads would've just come with me when I ran up north. Although they didn't listen to me I deeply admired the courage they had, the strength to which it took to stare down death without hesitation. There's a solace thought in them only doing it once while now we do it every day, I find comfort that they are in a better place free from the new world's demands. Giving the sign one last pat I continued on the empty road, pulling out my crumpled map revealed that I was only 2 exits away from the small town of Yurry, knowing once nightfall came I would need shelter from the cold and Yurry was made up of mostly brick buildings...buildings that I hope were still standing. I reached around to the side pocket of my backpack grabbing a small Wheat Bar, I had not eaten anything since burying

Ted and the fatigue from that decision was finally starting to wear on me, all I could do was shake my head in frustration as if I was attempting to shake off the thought of him. I looked back down at my feet silently patting against the straw-covered road hoping that the hypnotic movement would calm my mind of the unneeded thoughts. Suddenly a small rumble in the distance began to creep into the silence of the empty world, i stopped in my tracks, standing still so I could be sure of what I was hearing. My eyes danced around the scenery in front of me looking for what could be causing the unexpected noise. The rumbles seemingly getting louder I began to make my way off of the road into the side-brushed woods, hiding behind the thickness of the trees to wait out the abnormal noise. The sound drew even closer now revealing more to the confusing puzzle I was trying to solve in my head. It was a……car. My eyes began to widen as my heartbeat soon followed knowing that the only people who could afford the luxury of a car were the ones who went forth to take them along with the needed resources. I sat dead still in the brush of the woods waiting for the vehicle to pass me by, although I would love to get off my feet there was no way of knowing who was driving or why. My eyes locked onto the vehicle as it passed by showing a black painted body topped off with the small blue Ford logo and a red stripe on the rear corner panel…." no fucking way" feeling the panicked waves start to set through my body. I slowly emerged from the brush knowing that I needed to figure out where the voided crown vic was going. As I peered over the ditch I could see the car begin to turn right onto the same Yurry exit that I had planned to take. I frantically began rubbing my face with my hands as The thoughts I tried to close out quickly returned while being greeted by the new ones. The only people I knew with a red striped marking were the Marauders. Specific stripes helped them designate the usage of the scarce cars with red being a scout, scouts jobs were simple they would be sent out for weeks at a time looking for other groups or factions, and once they found one that seemed weak in their defensive efforts the marauders would come to fulfill their own wicked prophecies. "This doesn't make sense" whispering under my breath trying to gather some reason for the car's appearance. Once they had fully cleared out of view I stood to my feet, letting out an exhausted sigh. I wrestled with the thought of continuing into Yurry but there were too many questions that had to be answered. If this car indeed withheld a marauder scout it could lead me to a new community of people, one that hopefully wasn't infected by the same ruthless leaders I had come to know all too well.

Chapter 5 ***"The Descent Into Yurry"***

. Before the end, Yurry was one of those towns that would be deemed as "Vintage". there is a beauty to that, stepping back in time when things were a lot more simple, It wasn't filled with intersections or stoplights just a single-lane road with brick buildings surrounding it on both sides. Yurry invited people to slow down. To talk to each other, and walk with each other. An opportunity to stop time just for a moment. As the sun faded hiding Yurrys descent into chaos I could see a dimly lit flame illuminating from what used to be a donut shop. Moving quietly through the dead streets I made my way closer to the moss-covered building, slowly I peered my head into the window frame to see a man sitting around a small fire. He wore a large grey windbreaker and appeared to be focused on the journal he was holding. There was no doubt that this was the marauder I was looking for. He had too many bags and too much gear to be carrying it all by foot. Looking around I couldn't figure out where he had left the crown Vic, its all the more reason why they spray painted the cars black. Inching my way back into the window frame I couldn't believe what I was now seeing….." Isaiah?" the man jumped to his feet, caught off guard by my voice that had broken through the night's silence. "Isaiah, it's me…Ryan". The shocked look on his face began to fade now being replaced with confusion. Stepping out from behind the corners of the brick window frame, now looking directly at him. "What?...what..what the fuck are you doing here man" Searching for the answers to my surprise appearance, I was as shocked as he was. Isaiah was a friend from the marauder camp, we had known each other for over 2 years sharing many stories over our love for playing casino-based card games. "I uh…. I followed a journeyman to um…this gas station..and yea just kinda got lost.. it's a long story" giving him a piss poor excuse for why i was now here in Yurry, not really worrying about what he thought. Quickly I changed the subject "The better question is, when the hell did you become a scout?" Isaiah had always wanted to be a scout but usually Thorne wouldn't let anyone below 25 do anything he saw as important. "Ah

Dude..fucking Lauras crew got burnt hard" he was referring to one of the leaders of the scouting groups. "They put David in charge after that and you know David was gonna hook me up…so here i am scouting away" he let out a small laugh seemingly happy over his new role. "Probably gonna head back in the morning I'm sure you would enjoy getting off those worn-out ass feet.." moving deeper inside the building to sit on the small bucket Isaiah had given to me. I knew that I had to deter him from wanting me to ride back home with him. After all, Isaiah wasn't the brightest, failing to question me or even ask me more about my story. "No it's fine... I'm sure you're busy scouting out old casinos….or some shit" Isaiah let out a laugh "Actually I did find a place…and dude once I report all this back they will build statues of me" he responded with a confident tone underlined with brisk sarcasm. Joking about scouting the casinos was a form of asking him what he was doing in Yurry without exactly questioning him…" Oh so they got a complete chip set…what about some new cards?" I continued my sarcastic responses knowing that Isaiah would feel the need to explain himself further. "No in all seriousness…this is big..like I've never seen a place have so much yet have so little", "No watch towers, barely any walls, and the walls that are there are made from fucking tin roofs" I sat with a closed mouth listening to the details that he insisted on providing. I knew he felt strongly about his new find, he was very hopeful that this would impress Thorne further, helping him to submit himself to that trusted circle. "Listen dude ill even put in a good word for you. I'll tell those motherfuckers that you helped me with the find....shit it's a win for both of us" I started to feel a certain sorrow not only for this community that would eventually meet its demise but also for Isaiah, he was so caught up in the status of possibly being an authoritative figure for the marauders that he couldn't even realize what it would cost to do so. Countless lives would never get a chance to explain why they could live in harmony with people like us. "If we wiped out the journeymen that easy...then this shit will be a cakewalk. Basically a low risk - High reward" I stared off into the fire continuing to listen to Isaiah's ideas. "Plus on the brightside there's a ton of women and I mean hey free game right" he laughed, seemingly waiting for my response before going back into his speech. My Sorrow began turning into anger, I could feel the adrenaline start to come over, the thoughts of seeing the horrific acts before they were even done, and Isaiah continuing to find pride in being the one to set all of this into a reality. Fidgeting with my hands in an attempt to calm myself knowing that an outburst might reveal the depths of why I'm actually wondering around a random place like Yurry. With each word he spoke my mind became more clouded no longer hearing what he had to say, visions continuing to fill my head, questions coming faster than I could find the answers to. Suddenly I stood up pushing Isaiah off of the bucket seat onto the ground. Quickly I wrapped my hands around his neck squeezing with everything I had in me. He tried fighting me off his arms grasping into the air looking for something to pull himself out of this situation. “HE DIED BECAUSE OF YOU” Screaming into Isaiah's face I began lifting his head off of the ground slamming into the concrete floor over and over and over.....and over. Staring directly in his eyes I was finding joy in seeing this monster cling to the life that was no longer in his control. Slam after slam I could feel his grip on my arms beginning to loosen. “IM SORRY” “GODDAMN YOU” “IM SORRY” “YOU CANT DO THIS” my head becoming more clouded as finally isaiah's hands completely left my arms. I sat there looking at his now lifeless body. Letting go of him i fell back away from his body now breathing heavily as noticed by the winters air. “Im sorry” whispering as my eyes filled with uncontrollable tears....”im sorry”.....”im sorry”...continuing to express my remorse for Isaiah I lie down covering my face. “There was no choice…. FUCK, WHAT CHOICE DID YOU GIVE ME” hitting myself over the head i couldn't bear what had happen while simultaneously it felt like the right thing. It had to be the right thing. There was no other option right?.........

“JUST KILL ME”

CHAPTER 6 ***“Why God”***

I sat still for hours staring into the mossy-covered bricks, as the fire continued its dance against the walls. My Mind was Full of Racing thoughts but empty at the same time, looking into a void searching for a clearer sense of self that I knew I couldn't find. Reaching down into my bag, I picked out the 22 Revolver the same one that had taken teds life. My hands began to tremble as the racing thoughts started to clear giving me a pathway to what my own soul seemingly was begging me to do, tears began to fill my eyes yet again as it all became clearer. “no matter what buddy if you do not have hope then you don't have nothing” teds words echoed like a bad ambiance in my head, I finally had met the same crossroads my dear friend had met not long ago. Whispering under my breath

“Why have you forsaken me” a soft plea to god for help in a moment of uncertainty, not understanding why I was put in this position or even this very moment of life. My Cries began to get louder as the tears came down even heavier, scanning around the room as if I were looking for someone to pick me up off of the rubble-filled floor, my breathing rapidly increasing with each gnawing moment. “OH GOD, WHY” I screamed. My time had finally come, the overwhelming feelings were finally here to overpower me. No longer did I want to fight this world, but most importantly no longer did I want to fight myself. The visions and dreams I had to once again live in a world that was whole were fading away into what they were, to begin with…just a dream. Raising the revolver up to my head a slight smile began to creep across my face. I finally had clarity and knew what was gonna happen next, soon I would understand truly what it was like after the end. And if my faith held true I would shortly experience a life with no more pain…no more suffering. I wondered if that's how Ted felt in his final moments, maybe not an act of selfishness, just a way to forever escape this world's suffering. I opened my eyes one last time to just see everything to fully take in the moment. Noticing some small moths flying around the open flames of the fire, admiring the beauty of a bug I had never cared for before all of this. My eyes drifted away from the smoothness of the night down to isaiah's body, i dropped the revolver from my trembling hands down to the rocky floor. “No No No”..."WAKE UP RYAN PLEASE” i pleaded to myself. Climbing up off the floor and moving quickly to gather up the items I could, I knew then that i had to push forward, my life couldn't end here I had come too far. Soon the other scouts would come looking for Isaiah and along with his body, they would also stumble their way into the settlement he had found along his journey. Little did I know how much my life was about to change in a time when I was ready to draw the line. Grabbing the rest of Isaiah's gear and the hand-drawn map I set out in hopes of changing the destiny these people would soon face.

AFTER THE END

EXPLAINED

PREFACE PART 2

Now, That you have read the story I wanted to do something special for those who find depth in the book. As a person who loves explanations or deep dives on creative works I thought it would be a great experience to go through the book recalling and explaining certain moments. As you read there will be inserts from certain lines of the text explaining the ***WHY*** Behind the writing itself, How Characters were crafted and why certain storylines were chosen. There is a hidden beauty that the book was written over many different days, Many Different Emotions.

From Ryan pulling himself out of despair down to the moth itself that danced around the fire.

Enjoy

CHAPTER 1 *The World Is Yours*

(Chapter 1 is ONE of the Three Chapter that are actually Titled. The books focus on ryans mind is also supposed to reflect confusion and disarray on the reader..wondering why some are titled why some aren't.)

Did you ever think when we were watching all these stupid movies that something like this would ever happen? I let out a small laugh. My Sense of humor was one of the small things that I held onto, even when the world fell apart. "Well um" Ted paused and seemingly looked around the thin cool air of the

Night searching for an answer. "Hell, I guess not" Ted finished. It's odd to say but I have been enjoying,

The nighttime especially since I met Ted, maybe it was just the company of what appeared as a normal person.. I peered off into the night sky letting my thoughts and ideas run rampant like usual. It was almost like my therapy, a way to just “figure” it out,

Suddenly I let out a quick gasp that grabbed Ted's attention. Although thinking in silence helped me at times it could quickly get me shaken up too.

(Here Ryan has a mild panic attack, the idea came from my own “shaken” up moments. Often,when i would try to sleep at nights i would craft storys or storylines in my head, like playing a TV show in your own head. It was something that could always help me sleep but sometimes it wouldn't causing a small “Shaken” moment)

“What going on?” Ted hastily asked “Oh uh.. it's nothing I'm fine just..thought I saw something”

(Ryan Deflects Ted asking whats wrong with him, hes afraid to tell him but does not list why. Most of the time people hold things in. Whether lack of trust or other factors, ryan does the

same here, Sending the signal that ryan is closed off even though hes forming a bond with ted)

responding quickly so I wouldn't have to let Ted know that I had a mini panic attack. The world as I knew it was gone and that thought alone could make anyone go crazy. But no matter what I wanted to see through the destruction, the warfare I wanted to see through the terrible shit that people were doing to each other just to get by. I won't lie or pretend to be the perfect person or the shining knight in white armor because only god knows what I've also done to make it this far.

(These lines Reflect Ryan being a dreamer of sorts, the world is trashed, ruined and structure has fallen, yet he still wants to see through it. Funny enough these lines came from our own world. " I wanted to see through the terrible shit that people were doing to each other just to get by" is easily shown in today's society)

CHAPTER 2.

It had only been three days since I met Ted. We were both on the run from the constant gunfire of the major Tennessee Factions.
(Here we Start to figure out where this is all happening at. Due to me being from Alabama and only seeing a couple of states such as tennessee, i decided it was best to put this story in a place that i could see. The familiarity of the south helps me to craft the world building of the story. Later shown in Ryan going to Yurry, it just helps me connect more to the places were at)

It's funny to me that these groups of people could see everything we know and love destroyed by war just to continue it at a much smaller scale. After all, wiping out the electrical grid and more than half of the population wasn't enough to find different solutions to their disagreements.
(Honestly, Not sure where my headspace was on this day when writing it. But i do remember having some rage when

writing all this out. Its a "People Dont Stop until its to far gone" Kinda thing. A mix of personal and broader scale issues brought this in)

I had gotten word from an "outsider" days before I left that something was brewing between the two groups, not wanting to be around and help with another worthless killing I decided to leave. After all the group I claimed to were warmongers hell-bent on taking whatever they could just to come back home and share the bread that they never had to kill for in the first place.

(Another Example of anger at society, Ryan is seeking a justice that hes not sure exists anymore)

As for the other side well my group had met a match made in hell. 2 sides that didn't care who or why all they knew was that one had something the other didn't. While leaving that group I walked for days holding onto the hope that somewhere somehow people still cared about upholding what is right That was when I met Ted.

(Teds introduction plays him being from the "Other side" the side thats supposed to be Ryans Enemy. Furthermore these two meeting and creating some sort of friendship shows that

this failed world is now being run by people rushing to create there own and people like Ryan and Ted are just resources to push further)

Ted was from the opposite side a middle-aged man seemingly in search of the same things that I was looking for. Our first exposure was a run-down gas station withholding inside nothing but a glimpse into the final days of our normal world. Seeing the chaos of products that used to sit neatly on the shelf reduced to nothing but mere rubble gave me a feeling of lost hope.

(the gas station stems from a real life experience, off of a local highway sits a chain of abandoned gas stations and a lone diner. You can find the main gas station by inputting these coordinates into google maps - 31.277695402741358, - 87.20572640216483)

As I went to make a pallet to get some rest a man appeared from behind the checkout desk holding a long barrel 22 caliber revolver.

(Based off of the Heritage 22 Revolver.)

My heart sank just knowing that my final moments were upon me. "There is no need to do this" I blurted out the adrenaline-imposed response hoping that he would reason with me. The man crept closer towards me seemingly hesitant to get too close. he replied to me "Who are you and what do you want from here" Giving a stuttered yet quick response I told him "I'm just here to get some rest ok? That's all, I will leave" The man lowered the gun but kept his distance. A brief feeling of relief came over me. I had seen many people be killed without question. I knew at that moment the man was just safeguarding himself and that he also meant no harm. I slowly came up from my cardboard sleeping bag with my hands clear still hoping that he wouldn't change his mind last minute. "I'm just here for rest I promise I mean no harm to you" I assured him. He looked down at my bag seemingly looking for a weapon. "If you move towards that bag I will kill you," he told me as he looked into my eyes I could see the desperation of a man who didn't want to resort to taking my life.

("as he looked into my eyes I could see the desperation of a man who didn't want to resort to taking my life" This was important to note. Ted is presented just like most survivors in

other stories, but i wanted to make sure that he came off as more humane then the rest)

This intense meeting went on for what felt like hours. Usually it's best to not talk about where you are from but for the sake of finding common ground I told the man how I even ended up in this run-down gas station. Fast Forward 3 days later and now a Marauder and a Journeymen are sitting around a fire talking. Finding common ground and trust while running from the evils that now seemed to be behind them. I never thought in my wildest dreams that I would ever be able to reason with a member of the journeymen as sure as Ted thought the same from a Marauder. ***(The pacing is fast. I never wrote a story around what went on in those three days, leaving it up to the reader. Clearly they form a bond over the shared interest of rest)***

I found solace in Ted and talking about our experiences brought us all the closer as friends and now travelers. During our few nights together we would take turns feeding the flame that kept our warmth at night and this night was my turn to wake up and make sure we didn't freeze to death. But oddly Ted insisted that he would take care of the chore for tonight adding that I would love to get the extra sleep. as we lay down for the night I looked up into the ceiling of the gas station watching the flames illuminate and dance off and on from the broken particle boards.I then turned to my side and asked Ted “How did you manage to keep your humanity in all of this?” it was a question I asked myself a lot. Ted continued to rip up old stock boxes “Well in today's time buddy I think doing what's right is more valuable than the dollar was,” I thought on his answer which was right up the ally way of an old mentor part of the reason why I loved ted was his old school metaphors and responses he had ready to go at any time. “But why not shoot me you could have easily guaranteed yourself safety” I continued to dive deeper hoping that I could work up the courage to tell Ted about my own struggles without him seeing me in a different light. “Well buddy I could ask you the same question,” Ted replied. “Look I saw that you weren't looking for a fight..and that's another valuable currency to have” “I may not know you completely but I can see the hope you have…no matter what buddy if you do not have hope then you don't have nothing" ted Somley laughed at his response before tossing another piece of cardboard into the small burn barrel. I decided to take what Ted said and end the conversation there. Pondering on people's thoughts helped me get to sleep quicker so I told Ted goodnight and began to doze off. It was normal for me to have nightmares and right on cue they came. It was often nice to see my family again although the beauty never lasted long and I would soon be greeted by the same scene in which they met their fate. But just for a moment I got to see them all again, see them dancing and laughing just having fun. It was a reminder that wherever they were, it had to be a better place than here.

(Ryan Forms a bond here with Ted and Ted is now placed as a mentor figure to ryan. Ryan seeks to understand Ted to see if he can understand himself. This whole time ryans pushing for something more, Pushing for change but he doesn't understand why. Hes digging for his own answers from Ted ... .overall the goal of this was to give Ryan a confident or someone who gets him, someone who sees what he sees. Its a chance to be understood)

Quickly I woke up but not from my night terrors a gunshot had rang out echoing off the walls of the empty gas station. I grabbed my gun from my waist preparing for whatever lurked in the shadows. Frantically I scanned the scene of our sleeping area and saw that Ted was nowhere to be found .....

(Quick Snappy captures how fast things change, not only in this fiction world but in our own world. This scene is formed from being given bad news in my own life at such random times. From being woken up or whatever the case may be it always seemed to come in times of normality. The unexpected)

Chapter 3

I began moving slowly throughout the gas station with my gun drawn and my heart pumping. As I swept through the main shop floor seeing nothing more than the usual rubble and trash that covered the floor. From the corner, an open door stuck out it led to the bathroom and I could see what appeared to be a dimly lit candle flashing off the tile floor. Continuing a slow approach I peered around the open door where I could see a man sitting there. "Ted" I called out. Waiting a few moments for a response which did nothing but further the amount of stress I was under. Moving forward into the bathroom I grabbed the candle and using it as my light source revealed a lifeless body. It was Ted. My heart sank as I saw the blood that now covered the side of his face, looking down at his motionless hand sat the same 22. Revolver he had used to confront me at our first meeting. Seeing the man I had become so fond of in this state sent shockwaves through my body I began to breathe frantically in a state of panic that seemed to fight the truth of what had happened to Ted. ***(Teds death was built from my own dads death. Although ted was crafted from many people i had met his death serves as a sharp knife to ryan. Me and my own dad had a rocky relationship and when the news came it was like a knife to myself. I remember going from being flushed out to smiling because "I began to breathe frantically in a state of panic that seemed to fight the truth of what had happened to Ted" My body was fighting the truth of what had happen. Not being able to process the event)***

Quickly I stood up and began to search around from behind the bathroom door. Every step I took was greeted by the mashing of leftover glass and the solemn sounds of my pounding heart took an ambient noise to the leftover silence. I was sure that someone else was lurking in this gas station that we had called home. My Fear started to fade, being replaced with teeth-grinding rage.

(Ryans Mental Rollercoaster starts to shine here, but also him being in fight or flight mode. From Fear to Anger, almost like hes micro processing what's happened to Ted)

I stepped out from the open door frame beginning my descent into the darkness of the gas station. The anger fueled A moment where the realities of life and death were no more. All that mattered was finding the killer and avenging the death of the man I called a friend ignoring the dangers to myself. I stepped quickly through the dark room and began to call out to whatever lurked nearby "You motherfucker show yourself!" I began to clear all the vantage points that me and ted had marked out from our first night together. Moving closer to the stocking room I heard the sound of a box falling from its resting place onto the floor. Without an ounce of hesitation, I burst into the room and began firing. The intensity of the ringing filled my ears as flashes from my handgun's muzzle provided brief glimpses into what the room withheld. Before I knew it I had emptied the magazine into nothing more than a void. No one was there. I turned around and rushed from the stocking room back to Ted entering the bathroom for a second time just to still see what I didn't want to believe. The dawn sun was starting to creep in revealing more of teds fate and beside him I could see a folded piece of cardboard that read “Ryan”. .Briefly opening the folded cardboard letter the first sentence revealed that the man who took teds life was….ted. I closed the letter to cover my eyes all I could do was fall in defeat. Tears began streaming down my face. The very man who gave me hope seemingly had none left for himself.

(i used to really go out of my way to speak to others who seemed down. But ive always wanted to understand why i couldn't give my own self answers like i gave to them “The very man who gave me hope seemingly had none left for himself.” this line helps capture that)

I tucked away the cardboard letter in my pockets and just sat there with him. It was a surreal moment that made me reflect back on whether I should have opened up my own emotions to him instead of keeping them hidden. "What have I done" The thought ran in my head over and over that if I had just opened up my true sorrows to Ted maybe he would've never felt alone…or weak in his own thoughts. Beginning to move my head up towards the ceilings as if I was looking to god for the answers just to drop right back down searching for my own. The rising sun had now completely shown itself to the world signifying that a new day was here, wiping the steady tears I got up from the floor looking one last time at my lost friend.

(Again Ryans Mind is not in a good state. Not long ago he was just getting some rest, but now after Teds Death and the discovery of Ted's last moments the text cuts to "The rising sun had now completely shown itself to the world" embodying that he sat there for a long time lost in thought)

The Marauders saw burying the dead as a waste of time, usually just dragging the bodies outside of the fences to be burned or thrown into the wilderness because “Mother Nature has to eat too” something thorne always stressed to us while we left behind our fallen looters. I never believed in that but when you're prosecuted for questioning the leader sometimes silence is the best option…well the only option.

(no explanation needed here)

I walked outside to begin searching for the proper ground to bury Ted wanting to make sure his final resting place was something I could visit again, the backside of the gas station had a beautiful array of trees that seemingly served as an umbrella for the path leading into the woods. Off to the side stood a dogwood tree, although its flowers were not showing due to the winter I knew it would show its beautiful purity in the spring. In a world before chaos and destruction, I would always hear stories from my grandmother, about how the dogwood tree was used to make the cross Jesus was crucified on, and how god was upset with the use of the tree so he made sure that the trees never grew straight again. Giving them the true purity they deserved.

(My Grandmother passed away in 2021. She would've been ecstatic if i told her that i was writing a book. She was a good woman and She Loved God, i wanted to have something in this story to dedicate directly to her. Ryan Recalls his grandmother and he picks out the dogwood tree just because of her. One of my favorite moments in the book)

I brought Ted outside, wrapping him in my square stitched blanket making sure he was comfortable before lowering him down into his true last resting place. Part of me didn't want to leave his gravesite, so many thoughts filled my mind while I stood there looking at the freshly packed dirt. Almost as if a knife was being dug into my stomach pulling at everything inside of me to find the correct answers. The worst is not a question, but a "what if?". A glimpse into what could have been, and the reality of what will never be.

(Tying back to my own dads death and our rocky relationship. He was mostly out of my life more then in. I struggled with this as a kid,teenager and adult. Some days after his death I didn't

know if I was mourning him or what could have been. What should have been. "The worst is not a question, but a "what if?". A glimpse into what could have been, and the reality of what will never be" is directly written from my feelings about it all. One of if not the greatest lines i will ever write...in my own mind anyway00)

Chapter 4

I waited until the next morning to set back out from the gas station. The path forward was more clouded than the day I escaped from the marauder camp. It would be a lie for me to say I wanted to get back on the road again when in reality all I wanted to do was sleep, teds death had taken a toll that I hadn't felt since the world came crashing down.

(Ryans now entering a clear sense of disorientation. " the reality of what will never be.

")

Yeah, those awful days when the men in suits decided to let hell loose. I could remember the service announcement and the eerie feeling of that robotic voice when it told us we were under attack. Watching cities fall under the siege of bombs while America prepared for its final stand. I gripped the straps of my backpack tightly forcing myself to stop thinking about it, I couldn't afford to loathe about what had happened.

(i've been told that my lack of world building or backstory causes issues with the reading itself. But we're in Ryan's head. He also doesn't go over Ted's letter, much like he decides to stop thinking about the worlds grim fate. Ryan is trying to shut off these issues to push forward. He's putting dynamite in a bottle hoping it doesn't explode)

Looking up from my feet to see the long winding highway ahead of me I knew that it wouldn't be too much longer before I reached the Alabama State line. just the thought of getting there made me somewhat happy, after all, it was home and I hadn't been back since the great war. "God I hope this isn't a mistake" whispering to myself as the sign came into sight. With each step, I could feel the waves of uncertainty come over me, leaving guaranteed meals behind for a shot at a semi-normal life that was unheard of. I stopped in my tracks as the "Sweet Home Alabama" sign came within arms reach, it was pretty faded now no longer under upkeep by the workers who had helped make the world go around. Running my fingers across the bottom of the rusted sign gave me chills. I was home. A place my family never abandoned even as the world went to shit.

(i lead the story into my home state so i could again capture it much better then writing someplace i wasn't familiar with. Many times on rides in my local town I always see the city workers out and about doing upkeep on small things that make up the bigger picture. Such as flowers,signs and lights etc. and no matter where i've travelled to, it was always a big relief to the Sweet Home Alabama Sign come into view"

"You motherfuckers" shaking my head in sarcasm, wishing those hardheads would've just come with me when I ran up north.

Although they didn't listen to me I deeply admired the courage they had, the strength to which it took to stare down death without hesitation. There's a solace thought in them only doing it once while now we do it every day, I find comfort that they are in a better place free from the new world's demands. Giving the sign one last pat I continued on the empty road, pulling out my crumpled map revealed that I was only 2 exits away from the small town of Yurry, knowing once nightfall came I would need shelter from the cold and Yurry was made up of mostly brick buildings…buildings that I hope were still standing. I reached around to the side pocket of my backpack grabbing a small Wheat Bar, I had not eaten anything since burying Ted and the fatigue from that decision was finally starting to wear on me, all I could do was shake my head in frustration as if I was attempting to shake off the thought of him.

(it took me at least 2 hours to figure out what i would have Ryan eating. I think this was the longest worked chapter as the story's flow started to fade down. I actually researched how long and how easy it was to make a wheat bar 0_0. But again Ryan Continues to bottle up what hes going through opting to stay strong and push forward)

I looked back down at my feet silently patting against the straw-covered road hoping that the hypnotic movement would calm my mind of the unneeded thoughts.

(Storms. Alabama is known for bad weather..such as gusty winds, tornados etc. its earned the Dixie Ally tag time and time again. After severe weather comes here the roads are filled with straw, from the pine trees that cover the state. This helped build an environment to write on)

Suddenly a small rumble in the distance began to creep into the silence of the empty world, i stopped in my tracks, standing still so I could be sure of what I was hearing. My eyes danced around the scenery in front of me looking for what could be causing the unexpected noise. The rumbles seemingly getting louder I began to make my way off of the road into the side-brushed woods, hiding behind the thickness of the trees to wait out the abnormal noise. The sound drew even closer now revealing more to the confusing puzzle I was trying to solve in my head. It was a……car. My eyes began to widen as my heartbeat soon followed knowing that the only people who could afford the luxury of a car were the ones who went forth to take them along with the needed resources. I sat dead still in the brush of the woods waiting for the vehicle to pass me by, although I would love to get off my feet there was no way of knowing who was driving or why. My eyes locked onto the vehicle as it passed by showing a black painted body topped off with the small blue Ford logo and a red stripe on the rear corner panel...." no fucking way" feeling the panicked waves start to set through my body. I slowly emerged from the brush knowing that I needed to figure out where the voided crown vic was going.

(giving some humor to this, the Ford Crown Vic was chosen because those cars seemingly run forever. Most of the time they are former police cruisers that were auctioned off so being in a black or white color. Next time you're out and about take a second to count just how many crown vics you see on the road...trust me there's alot more then you would think)

As I peered over the ditch I could see the car begin to turn right onto the same Yurry exit that I had planned to take. I frantically began rubbing my face with my hands as The thoughts I tried to close out quickly returned while being greeted by the new ones. The only people I knew with a red striped marking were the Marauders.

Specific stripes helped them designate the usage of the scarce cars with red being a scout, scouts jobs were simple they would be sent out for weeks at a time looking for other groups or factions, and once they found one that seemed weak in their defensive efforts the marauders would come to fulfill their own wicked prophecies. “This doesn't make sense” whispering under my breath trying to gather some reason for the car's appearance. Once they had fully cleared out of view I stood to my feet, letting out an exhausted sigh. I wrestled with the thought of continuing into Yurry but there were too many questions that had to be answered. If this car indeed withheld a marauder scout it could lead me to a new community of people, one that hopefully wasn't infected by the same ruthless leaders I had come to know all too well.

(This is where you see more of the world being built, Ryan never tells the full story on his former group. He doesn't want to relive anything, but here we see him fully explain the marauder scouts to the reader. I know i know its all hard to understand, but this book reflects his mind in many avenues that go right back toward a reader. Recall back to earlier where hes talking about the worlds fall, he tells the reader some pieces but its quickly shut off. Why? Because ryan doesn't

want to confront the past he wants to keep moving forward, so when these bad thoughts arise he's afraid dwelling on them will halt his progress or his hope for something better. He just wants to move forward.)

Chapter 5

. Before the end, Yurry was one of those towns that would be deemed as "Vintage". there is a beauty to that, stepping back in time when things were a lot more simple, It wasn't filled with intersections or stoplights just a single-lane road with brick buildings surrounding it on both sides. Yurry invited people to slow down. To talk to each other, and walk with each other. An opportunity to stop time just for a moment.

(Yurry is based off of two Alabama Towns. The First one being Brewton, Alabama and The Other Being Enterprise Alabama. If you would like to view the 2 streets used here are the google

map coordinates. Enterprise - 31.314172560469046, -85.85376821602587 Brewton - 31.10416605840794, -87.0719177842358)

As the sun faded hiding Yurrys descent into chaos I could see a dimly lit flame illuminating from what used to be a donut shop. Moving quietly through the dead streets I made my way closer to the moss-covered building, slowly I peered my head into the window frame to see a man sitting around a small fire. He wore a large grey windbreaker

(The Grey Windbreaker was used simply because my sister had gotten me a grey windbreaker for christmas, still all the more interesting that even little details stem from real life things)

and appeared to be focused on the journal he was holding. There was no doubt that this was the marauder I was looking for. He had too many bags and too much gear to be carrying it all by foot. Looking around I couldn't figure out where he had left the crown Vic, its all the more reason why they spray painted the cars black. Inching my way back into the window frame I couldn't believe what I was now seeing….." Isaiah?" the man jumped to his feet, caught off guard by my voice that had broken through the night's silence. “Isaiah, it's me…Ryan”. The shocked look on his face began to fade now being replaced with confusion. Stepping out from behind the corners of the brick window frame, now looking directly at him. “What?...what..what the fuck are you doing here man” Searching for the answers to my surprise appearance, I was as shocked as he was. Isaiah was a friend from the marauder camp, we had known each other for over 2 years sharing many stories over our love for playing casino-based card games

“I uh…. I followed a journeyman to um…this gas station..and yea just kinda got lost.. it's a long story” giving him a piss poor excuse for why i was now here in Yurry, not really worrying about what he thought. Quickly I changed the subject “The better question is, when the hell did you become a scout?” Isaiah had always wanted to be a scout but usually Thorne wouldn't let anyone below 25 do anything he saw as important.

"Ah Dude..fucking Lauras crew got burnt hard" he was referring to one of the leaders of the scouting groups. "They put David in charge after that and you know David was gonna hook me up…so here i am scouting away"

(Another Small Detail with names here, David is a Friend of mine that i met through gaming. Isaiah is a name from a childhood friend. Ted was the name of my Papa or the broader used term, Grandfather)

he let out a small laugh seemingly happy over his new role. "Probably gonna head back in the morning I'm sure you would enjoy getting off those worn-out ass feet.." moving deeper inside the building to sit on the small bucket Isaiah had given to me. I knew that I had to deter him from wanting me to ride back home with him. After all, Isaiah wasn't the brightest, failing to question me or even ask me more about my story."No it's fine... I'm sure you're busy scouting out old casinos….or some shit" Isaiah let out a laugh "Actually I did find a place…and dude once I report all this back they will build statues of me" he responded with a confident tone underlined with brisk sarcasm. Joking about scouting the casinos was a form of asking him what he was doing in Yurry without exactly questioning him…" Oh so they got a complete chip set…what about some new cards?" I continued my sarcastic responses knowing that Isaiah would feel the need to explain himself further.

(Ryan uses his depth to basically manipulate Isaiah into giving him more answers, a darker theme of the character that i originally wanted to explore more)

"No in all seriousness…this is big..like I've never seen a place have so much yet have so little", "No watch towers, barely any walls, and the walls that are there are made from fucking tin roofs" I sat with a closed mouth listening to the details that he insisted on providing. I knew he felt strongly about his new find, he was very hopeful that this would impress Thorne further, helping him to submit himself to that trusted circle. "Listen dude ill even put in a good word for you. I'll tell those motherfuckers that you helped me with the find….shit it's a win for both of us" I started to feel a certain sorrow not only for this community that would eventually meet its demise but also for Isaiah, he was so caught up in the status of possibly being an authoritative figure for the marauders that he couldn't even realize what it would cost to do so. Countless lives would never get a chance to explain why they could live in harmony with people like us.

(Ryans Visionary Outlook shines through here ALOT, he's thinking about people he doesn't even know and what could possibly happen to them. Ryans mind is tormented not only with his own problems but the problems of others)

“If we wiped out the journeymen that easy…then this shit will be a cakewalk. Basically a low risk - High reward” I stared off into the fire continuing to listen to Isaiah's ideas. “Plus on the brightside there's a ton of women and I mean hey free game right” he laughed, seemingly waiting for my response before going back into his speech. My Sorrow began turning into anger, I could feel the adrenaline start to come over, the thoughts of seeing the horrific acts before they were even done, and Isaiah continuing to find pride in being the one to set all of this into a reality. Fidgeting with my hands in an attempt to calm myself knowing that an outburst might reveal the depths of why I'm actually wandering around a random place like Yurry. With each word he spoke my mind became more clouded no longer hearing what he had to say, visions continuing to fill my head, questions coming faster than I could find the answers to. Suddenly I stood up pushing Isaiah off of the bucket seat onto the ground. Quickly I wrapped my hands around his neck squeezing with everything I had in me.

(Ryan has fought back bad thoughts this whole story with the goal of pushing forward and doing the right thing. Here we see him overload, a symptom of bottling up emotions with no where to put them)

He tried fighting me off his arms grasping into the air looking for something to pull himself out of this situation. "HE DIED BECAUSE OF YOU" Screaming into Isaiah's face I began lifting his head off of the ground slamming into the concrete floor over and over and over.....and over. Staring directly in his eyes I was finding joy in seeing this monster cling to the life that was no longer in his control. Slam after slam I could feel his grip on my arms beginning to loosen. "IM SORRY" "GODDAMN YOU" "IM SORRY" "YOU CANT DO THIS" my head becoming more clouded as finally isaiah's hands completely left my arms. I sat there looking at his now lifeless body. Letting go of him i fell back away from his body now breathing heavily as noticed by the winters air. "Im sorry" whispering as my eyes filled with uncontrollable tears...."im sorry"....."im sorry"...continuing to express my remorse for Isaiah I lie down covering my face. "There was no choice.... FUCK, WHAT CHOICE DID YOU GIVE ME" hitting myself over the head i couldn't bear what had happen while simultaneously it felt like the right thing. It had to be the right thing. There was no other option right?.........

"JUST KILL ME"

(This Scene is Graphic and a little insane honestly. The goal was for it to read like its well...insane. Like a man loosing grip of his own mind. We know that Ryan Carries a Weapon but instead he chooses to use his own hands this further makes the scene more gruesome, More.....angry)

CHAPTER 6 "Why God"

(why god is my favorite chapter, so many elements of my own life, was put into making ryans stand with himself feel...real. The Book is Mimicking his Mind and here in "Why God" we see him have a very manic and real switch from anger to a dark sadness)

I sat still for hours staring into the moss-covered bricks, as the fire continued its dance against the walls. My Mind was Full of Racing thoughts but empty at the same time, looking into a void searching for a clearer sense of self that I knew I couldn't find. Reaching down into my bag, I picked out the 22 Revolver, the same one that had taken Ted's life. My hands began to tremble as the racing thoughts started to clear, giving me a pathway to what my own soul seemingly was begging me to do, tears began to fill my eyes yet again as it all became clearer. “no matter what buddy if you do not have hope then you don't have nothing” teds words echoed like a bad ambiance in my head, I finally had met the same crossroads my dear friend had met not long ago. Whispering under my breath
“Why have you forsaken me?”

(In the bible Jesus says the exact line “Why have you forsaken me?”. I used it not to disrespect jesus, but because i had used it in my own life when I had run out of words. Finally coming to the end of my own rope I simply asked “Why have you forsaken me?” You see this reflected in my writing as a soft plea to god ... .a cry for help. I think it's a beautiful moment

showing that Ryan is still fighting, he's still talking to God asking for a hand. He hasn't given up just yet.)

a soft plea to god for help in a moment of uncertainty, not understanding why I was put in this position or even this very moment of life. My Cries began to get louder as the tears came down even heavier, scanning around the room as if I were looking for someone to pick me up off of the rubble-filled floor, my breathing rapidly increasing with each gnawing moment. "OH GOD, WHY" I screamed. My time had finally come, the overwhelming feelings were finally here to overpower me. No longer did I want to fight this world, but most importantly no longer did I want to fight myself. The visions and dreams I had to once again live in a world that was whole were fading away into what they were, to begin with…just a dream. Raising the revolver up to my head a slight smile began to creep across my face. I finally had clarity and knew what was going to happen next, soon I would understand truly what it was like after the end. And if my faith held true I would shortly experience a life with no more pain…no more suffering. I wondered if that's how Ted felt in his final moments, maybe not an act of selfishness, just a way to forever escape this world's suffering. I opened my eyes one last time to just see everything to fully take in the moment. Noticing some small moths flying around the open flames of the fire, admiring the beauty of a bug I had never cared for before all of this. ***(“admiring the beauty of a bug I had never cared for before all of this.” the scene with the moth is REAL. but in a different way. One day i was feeling very upset and decided to go for a drive just to think. I stopped at a local bridge that i stop at regularly just to take a look at the water. But this time i was just sitting there staring...like i was looking for answers in this muddy river. A piece of wood came floating by and my eyes locked onto it, it was pretty to me at that moment. Most of the time it would've been something ignored but not this time, Finding Beauty in something i had never cared for before all of this)***

My eyes drifted away from the smoothness of the night down to isaiah's body, i dropped the revolver from my trembling hands down to the rocky floor. “No No No”..."WAKE UP RYAN PLEASE” i pleaded to myself. Climbing up off the floor and moving quickly to gather up the items I could, I knew then that i had to push forward, my life couldn't end here I had come too far. Soon the other scouts would come looking for Isaiah and along with his body, they would also stumble their way into the settlement he had found along his journey. Little did I know how much my life was about to change in a time when I was ready to draw the line. Grabbing the rest of Isaiah's gear and the hand-drawn map I set out in hopes of changing the destiny these people would soon face.

(the story doesn't give a real reason why Ryan decides to keep moving forward, other then the care he has for the people of Yurry. I end the story not guaranteeing anything for Ryan, the only thing we see is he abruptly gets up and gets going. Yet again the reader sees the state of his mind, circle right back to him not wanting to continue with stories of the fall or recalling his family completely. Time and time again Ryan pushes hurtful thoughts away to just move forward and here we see how fine the line really is for him.

Much like the preface, I hope this book helps someone. Whether that's putting words to your own thoughts or seeing something you relate to and saying "hey this person

understands me" alot of the time we all think we're alone in our own thoughts, that no ones understands but you would be surprised to know that there are people who do understand. I'm not guaranteeing you tomorrow will be better than yesterday but i am guaranteeing you that you do matter even if today doesn't feel like it. Dont let this world beat you down. Keep Pushing Forward even if the reasons to do so aren't clear, there is a Yurry out there for all of us.)

After The End Early Concepts and Forgotten Ideas

Now that you've wrapped up After The End and The Explanations Story, I would like to go into how the book was finally completed, when I knew to wrap it up into the short book you know. Originally, I planned for After The End to be much, much longer with a more broad storyline that followed a somewhat traditional sense of writing. So here is After The End's Early Concepts and Forgotten Ideas. Enjoy.

Teds Letter was to be revealed at the end of the book

Originally, I planned to create a full circle moment with Ted's letter. Ryan never addressed this, and it was deliberate to do so. Even with the letter not being mentioned in this book's ending, it leaves room for it to make an even bigger impact in a sequel. Still, it all worked out as I was able to tie in Ted's .22 Revolver to Ryan's final stand and make sure that Ted was still a direct thought of Ryan's.

Isaiah Wasn't intended to be Ryans Target

Ryan was supposed to have a run-in with one of the main faces behind the Marauders faction, not Isaiah. This would introduce readers to the villains Ryan recalls in the story, intended to have heavy dialogue where we explored more of what it's like in the Marauders' world. Instead, I opted for Isaiah. With him being a former friend of Ryan, the impact to me was just different; it was more than just your average villain.

Ryan Arrives At Yurry

When Ryan arrives at Yurry, it was meant to be the light at the end of the tunnel. He would finally come across a place still grounded in the morals and laws of the world before. This chapter was actually supposed to be where he started to question his own life. After finally finding the place he was looking for, he would question whether he deserved it or not, further diving into Ryan's tormented mind.

The Marauders Invade Yurry

With the Marauders invading Yurry, they would take out their leader as well. After successfully defending against the Marauder invasion, Yurry would look toward a new leader, and that's where they would find Ryan to be the next person in charge. He knew the Marauders and how they operated, giving him more trust but at the same time distrust from the people in Yurry.

Ryans Descent Into Darkness

As the leader of Yurry, we would expect Ryan to uphold his moral code and steer the community in the ways he reflected on in the final story, but he doesn't. Instead, Ryan becomes so hell-bent on wiping out the Marauders that he's blind to the damage he does to Yurry itself. He starts operating much like the Marauders did.

So why didn't these storylines stick?

The story no longer aligned with my original vision when I began writing. I wanted it to be raw, honest, and filled with emotions I hadn't seen captured so precisely in other books. I wrote the first five chapters from November to mid-December before setting the project aside entirely. My goal was for the book to be at least a novella, but I couldn't continue writing from what felt like an inauthentic perspective. In April 2025, during another difficult period in my life, I started thinking about channeling those emotions back into the book. After a few days of reflection, I decided I didn't care about word count or adhering to traditional expectations; I just wanted to finish the story as I had intended. That's when I wrote the chapter "Why God."

AFTER THE ENDS

RELEASE

STORY

When I published the book on Amazon's KDP program, I genuinely didn't have any high expectations for it—none at all—and I was okay with that because I loved the story myself. Even if others didn't, it wouldn't have changed my mind. Sure, it's rough around the edges and could be polished throughout, but it's genuine, and it's something I put a lot of time into, carefully creating and capturing true, raw emotions. So, when four days after the book's release I saw it on the top 100 charts for Teen and Young Adult Short Reads, I was more than shocked—I was actually happy. I felt like maybe I did do something right here, maybe my message was being heard. This was a rare moment for me. Most of the time, when I'm making or creating something, whether it be a video or something completely random, I'm never satisfied with the end result. I'm always mad at myself, feeling like I could have done better, but this was different. I think even if the book never touched a single chart in its life, I could still look back and enjoy what I put into making it.

SO WHAT

NOW?

I plan to continue "After the End." As of right now, in this moment, I have no clear idea of what the sequel will look like, but I do know that I want to give this story even more. Just like in the explanations section of this book, I find myself lying down at night, envisioning how the story unfolds, who Ryan becomes, what he faces, and what he deals with as we now truly begin to explore this ruined world.

Building a Community

If you want to share your ideas, thoughts, or lore about the book itself, consider joining one of our online communities.

For Links To Our Community servers such as discord or reddit send "YES" to AfterTheEnd2025@Gmail.com

For EBook Users Simply Copy and Paste These Links into your browser

Discord - https://discord.gg/aQjPdMG2Rt

Reddit - https://www.reddit.com/r/AfterTheEndShortNovel/

Made in the USA
Columbia, SC
10 May 2025

57639824R00046